The 3-D Library of the Human Body

THE LUNGS
LEARNING HOW WE BREATHE

Chris Hayhurst

the rosen publishing group's
rosen
central

Editor's Note

The idea for the illustrations in this book originated in 1986 with the Vesalius Project at Colorado State University's Department of Anatomy and Neurobiology. There, a team of scientists and illustrators dreamed of turning conventional two-dimensional anatomical illustrations into three-dimensional computer images that could be rotated and viewed from any angle, for the benefit of students of medicine and biology. In 1988 this dream became the Visible Human Project™, under the sponsorship of the National Library of Medicine in Bethesda, Maryland. A grant was awarded to the University of Colorado School of Medicine, and in 1993 the first work of dissection and scanning began on the body of a Texas convict who had been executed by lethal injection. The process was repeated on the body of a Maryland woman who had died of a heart attack. Applying the latest techniques of computer graphics, the scientific team was able to create a series of three-dimensional digital images of the human body so beautiful and startlingly accurate that they seem more in the realm of art than science. On the computer screen, muscles, bones, and organs of the body can be turned and viewed from any angle, and layers of tissue can be electronically peeled away to reveal what lies underneath. In reproducing these digital images in two-dimensional print form, the editors at Rosen have tried to preserve the three-dimensional character of the work by showing organs of the body from different perspectives and using illustrations that progressively reveal deeper layers of anatomical structure.

Published in 2002 by The Rosen Publishing Group, Inc.
29 East 21st Street, New York, NY 10010

Digital anatomy images published by arrangement with Anatographica, LLC.
216 East 49th Street, New York, NY 10017

First Edition

Library of Congress Cataloging-in-Publication Data

Hayhurst, Chris.
The Lungs: learning how we breathe / Chris Hayhurst.
p. cm. — (The 3-D library of the human body)
Includes bibliographical references and index.
Summary: Discusses the anatomy and functioning of the lungs, how we breathe, and how oxygen is brought to the cells of the body.
ISBN 0-8239-3534-5
1. Lungs—Juvenile literature. [1. Lungs. 2. Respiration.]
I. Title. II. Series.
QP121 .H358 2001
612.2—dc21
                                                                2001003171

Manufactured in the United States of America

CONTENTS

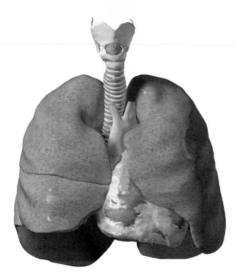

PREFACE
AN OBSESSION WITH CLEANLINESS

Before the second half of the nine-teenth century, the joke that "the operation was successful but the patient died" was no laughing matter. Fifty percent of hospital patients who survived surgery died of postoperative infection. In the public's mind, the hospital was simply a layover on the way to the morgue. Those who could afford to, hired private doctors and were treated at home, praying that their illnesses were not serious enough to warrant a trip to the operating room.

All of this was changed by British surgeon Joseph Lister (1827–1912). Lister earned his medical degree from the University of London in 1852. In 1856, he was appointed to the Edinburgh Royal Infirmary, and in 1861 he became a surgeon at the Glasgow Royal Infirmary. Lister was a deeply religious and humble man who had no interest in financial or social success, but he was very concerned about the high death rates in his hospital. He reported that between 1861 and 1865, almost half of his patients who had a limb amputated died of infection, and there seemed to be little that he or other doctors could do about it.

Lister noticed that some injuries, like simple bone fractures where the skin was not broken, did not suffer from infection the way open wounds did. He thought that particles in the air, "disease dust" as they were called, got into the open wounds and caused infections. He was moving in the right direction. In 1865, he began to read reports about the work of Louis Pasteur (1822–1895) in France and Pasteur's "germ theory of disease." Pasteur claimed that microscopic living organisms could cause decay of tissues, just as they could cause fermentation in wine and beer.

Lister became a passionate advocate of Pasteur's ideas. He insisted upon absolute cleanliness in the operating theater, including the sterilization of surgical instruments and patients' wounds with carbolic acid. When closing wounds, Lister applied bandages soaked in carbolic acid. At first, the nurses resented all of the extra work, and other doctors scoffed at his strange ideas about invisible infectious agents. But between 1865 and 1869, the postsurgical death rate at the Glasgow Royal Infirmary dropped to 15 percent. In 1867, Lister was able to report to the British Medical Association that no patient had died of infection for a period of nine months.

By the 1870s, Lister's fame was growing, and doctors as far away as Germany were introducing antiseptic methods into the operating theater. In 1878, German bacteriologist Robert Koch (1843–1910) demonstrated the use of steam to sterilize surgical instruments. Antiseptics less corrosive than carbolic acid were soon found. But as far as London doctors were concerned, Glasgow was a provincial backwater, and they wanted more proof. In 1877, Lister came to teach at King's College. On October 26 of that year, he operated on a patient with a fractured kneecap, an injury that often resulted in postoperative infection and death. Lister performed the surgery under antiseptic conditions, and the patient survived. The medical establishment was won over. Lister received many honors and was eventually knighted.

As a result of Lister's work, hospitals were no longer seen as places to go to die, and more and more people began to take advantage of their services. Even today, when doctors and surgeons talk about the history of hospital care, they will talk about surgery "Before Lister" and "After Lister."

1
THE LUNGS

The human body is a complex piece of machinery. It is so complex, in fact, that medical scientists and biologists—the people who study the body day in and day out—still don't know everything about it. They have questions, for example, about how the brain deals with love. And they wonder why some people are more likely than others to develop certain diseases or excel at particular professions.

What scientists do know, however, is that without oxygen, no part of the body—not the brain, the heart, the legs, the arms, or anything else—would work. More than any other elements, we need oxygen, which is found in nature as a component of air, to survive. With oxygen, the trillions of cells that make up the individual building blocks of the body can live. Without it, they die.

The process by which oxygen is supplied to all living cells is called respiration, and the body system that controls this process is called the respiratory system. The primary body organs used in respiration are the two lungs, but other body parts—including the brain, the wall of the chest, and several muscles—also play very important roles.

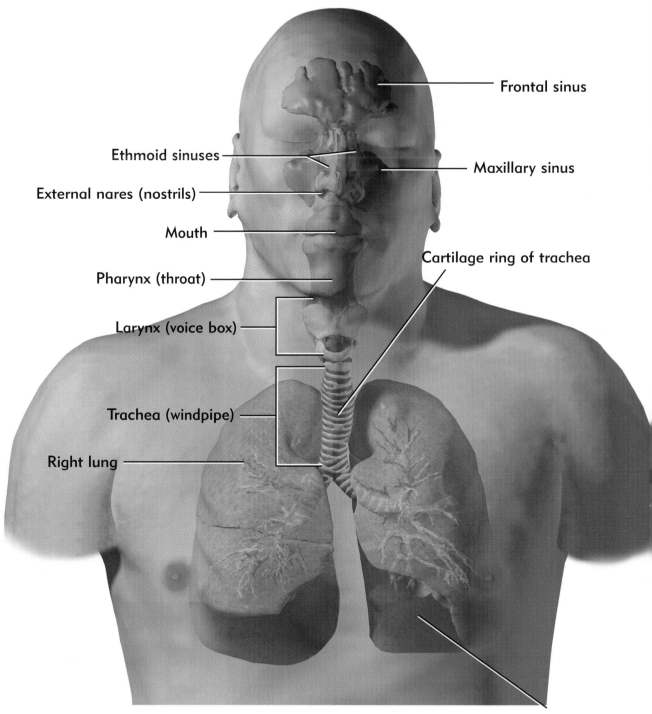

Frontal sinus

Ethmoid sinuses

Maxillary sinus

External nares (nostrils)

Mouth

Cartilage ring of trachea

Pharynx (throat)

Larynx (voice box)

Trachea (windpipe)

Right lung

Left lung

The respiratory system provides the body with oxygen, which is used by the cells to burn glucose and release energy.

Respiratory Anatomy

The lungs themselves are quite ordinary looking. Light pink in color, they are big as organs go, but because they're full of air they weigh surprisingly little. They take up most of the space in the thoracic cavity, or chest, and, because they come in pairs, they are referred to as "left" and "right." The left lung lies within the left half of the chest cavity, just to the left of the heart. The right lung is just to the right of the heart. The heart and the major blood vessels that connect to it are separated from the lungs by a thin bag of protective tissue called the mediastinum.

Each lung is divided into visible lobes, or sections, by deep, rounded grooves called fissures. The right lung has three lobes, while the left has only two. Anatomists refer to the superior, or top, part of each lung, where it is most narrow, as the apex. The apex is located just behind the clavicle, which you probably know as the collarbone. The flat inferior, or bottom, side of the lung is referred to as the base. The base sits on the diaphragm, an important muscle used in breathing.

Surrounding the lungs on their outer surfaces are two layers of wax-paperlike tissue called pleurae. The innermost layer of tissue, which attaches to the lungs, is known as the visceral pleura. The outer layer, which lines the internal chest walls, is called the parietal pleura. A narrow open region called the interpleural space separates the two pleural layers and is filled with a slippery fluid. The pleural fluid acts like a lubricant and allows the pleural layers to slip and slide back and forth over each other. At the same time, it causes the two layers to cling to one another, much like two panes of glass might stick together when wet. This means the lungs essentially cling to the internal walls of the chest, so when your chest expands, such as when you begin to take a breath of air, your lungs expand, too.

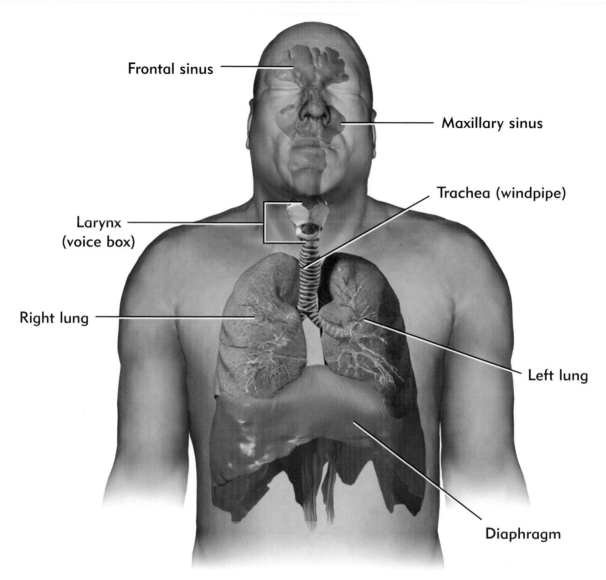

Frontal sinus

Maxillary sinus

Trachea (windpipe)

Larynx
(voice box)

Right lung

Left lung

Diaphragm

The lungs take up most of the space in the thoracic cavity. The diaphragm is a large, dome-shaped muscle that moves up and down to expand or contract the lungs.

To understand the inside of the lungs it helps to know a little about how they connect to the outside world. Respiration is made possible by the act of breathing. When we breathe, we pull air, and the oxygen that's in it, down a series of passageways that lead to the lungs. These passageways serve several purposes: to direct the air to the lungs and to filter, moisten, and warm the air before it gets there.

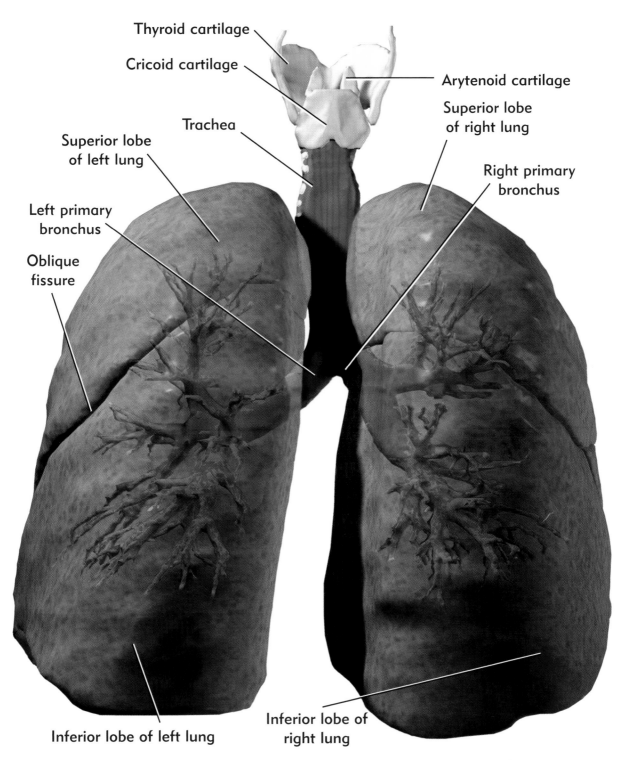

Thyroid cartilage

Cricoid cartilage

Arytenoid cartilage

Trachea

Superior lobe of right lung

Superior lobe of left lung

Right primary bronchus

Left primary bronchus

Oblique fissure

Inferior lobe of left lung

Inferior lobe of right lung

This is a posterior (rear) view of the lungs. Each lung is divided into lobes by deep grooves called fissures. The right lung has three, while the left has only two.

You're probably well acquainted with the first two passageways. The nose and the mouth are the entrance points for air. Air enters the nose through the nostrils, which anatomists call the external nares. Beyond the nostrils is the nasal cavity. The walls of the nasal cavity are lined with mucous membranes. Glands in the mucous membranes produce a sticky substance called mucus which moistens the air as it passes by and traps much of the microscopic dirt and bacteria that is in it. Veins, which carry blood to the heart, branch like a web directly behind the mucous membranes. The warm blood in the veins acts like a heater for the nearby mucus, which in turn transfers some of that heat to the air as it passes by.

The nasal cavity is surrounded by a number of hollow spaces within the skull called sinuses. The sinuses serve several purposes. Because they're essentially empty chambers, they make the skull lighter. They also secrete more mucus, which leaks into the nasal cavities to join the mucus created there.

The passageway below the mouth and the nasal cavity is known as the pharynx, or throat. Both food from the mouth and air from the mouth or nose travels down the pharynx. The pharynx has three main parts. The uppermost part is called the nasopharynx. This is the nasal connector— where air from the nasal cavity enters the pharynx. Inferior to the nasopharynx is the oropharynx, the oral part of the pharynx. Air and food from the mouth travel through the oropharynx, as does air from the nose that has already passed through the nasopharynx. The last part of the pharynx, located inferior to the oropharynx, is the laryngopharynx. The entire pharynx, including all three of its parts, is around five inches long in the average adult.

Inferior to and continuous with the pharynx is the larynx, or voice box. It's called the voice box because it houses the vocal cords, which are used in speaking. The larynx is formed by eight pieces of rigid cartilage, but its most obvious feature is the shieldlike thyroid cartilage, or "Adam's

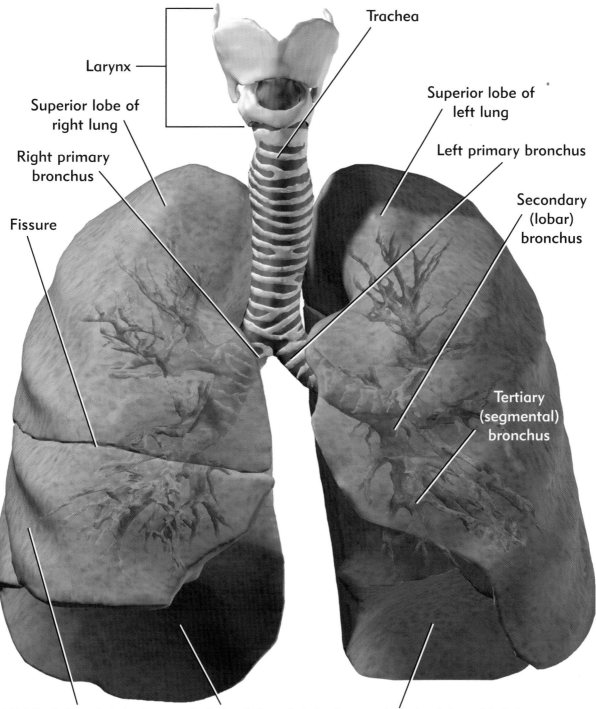

Trachea

Larynx

Superior lobe of right lung

Right primary bronchus

Fissure

Superior lobe of left lung

Left primary bronchus

Secondary (lobar) bronchus

Tertiary (segmental) bronchus

Middle lobe of right lung   Inferior lobe of right lung   Inferior lobe of left lung

This is an anterior (front) view of the lungs. Air is inhaled and moves through the trachea and bronchi. The bronchi branch out into even smaller passageways within the lungs. The smallest passageways are called bronchioles.

apple." The larynx is the "gatekeeper" for the remaining passageways to the lungs. Its main job, made possible by a flap of elastic cartilage at its top end called the epiglottis, is to make sure that only air—and not food or liquids—can enter. When you swallow, the larynx is pulled upward and the epiglottis tips to form a protective lid over its opening. When you're not swallowing, and are just breathing, the epiglottis does not block the opening to the larynx. The lid forces food and liquids to travel down the esophagus toward the stomach and keeps them from going down the trachea, which is the main airway. If anything other than air does somehow make it into the larynx, a cough reflex usually forces it back up.

Air from the larynx travels down and into the trachea, or windpipe. The trachea is about four inches long in the average adult. Like the larynx, it's rigid and reinforced with C-shaped strips of cartilage, which you can feel when you tilt your head back and rub the ventral part (toward the front) of your neck. The open end of the C, on the dorsal side (toward the back) where there is no cartilage, borders the esophagus and allows the esophagus to expand when you swallow.

At the bottom of the trachea, the airway branches into two major tubes called the left and right main bronchi. The right bronchus leads to the right lung. The left bronchus leads to the left lung. Within the lungs, the bronchi branch into smaller and smaller bronchi. It's a lot like a main tree branch dividing into smaller branches. The smallest of the bronchi branches (like twigs) are called bronchioles.

The last of the air-conducting bronchioles are called terminal bronchioles. They, in turn, split into even smaller branches called respiratory bronchioles. The respiratory bronchioles eventually end at microscopic air sacs called alveoli, where gas exchange between the lungs and blood takes place. Scientists estimate that the average lung has around 300 million alveoli.

2
BREATHING

Go ahead—take a deep breath. Feel the air as it rushes down your throat and fills your lungs. Hold it there for a second. Now, release. Let the air pour out, all the way out. Let your body relax. OK. Now, stop. Don't breathe in. Just wait. How long did you last? If you're like most people, you probably were able to hold your breath for a few seconds. Then, because you absolutely had to—you didn't have a choice—you inhaled again.

Breathing is automatic. Because your body needs oxygen to survive, it also tells you when you have to breathe. In fact, it's the brain that controls your basic breathing rhythm and how much air you take in with each breath. The brain receives signals from special receptors in the heart and the carotid artery (the big blood vessel in the neck) when oxygen levels in the blood begin to drop and when carbon dioxide levels begin to rise. In response to those signals, the brain sends a separate message down the spinal cord to nerves that connect to the muscles of the respiratory system. When the muscles finally get the order, they immediately kick into gear and start the actual breathing process.

Inhalation, or "inspiration" as it's also known, is the first mechanical stage of the breathing process. It begins when the diaphragm, a narrow, dome-shaped muscle positioned immediately below the lungs, and the intercostal muscles, which are located between each rib,

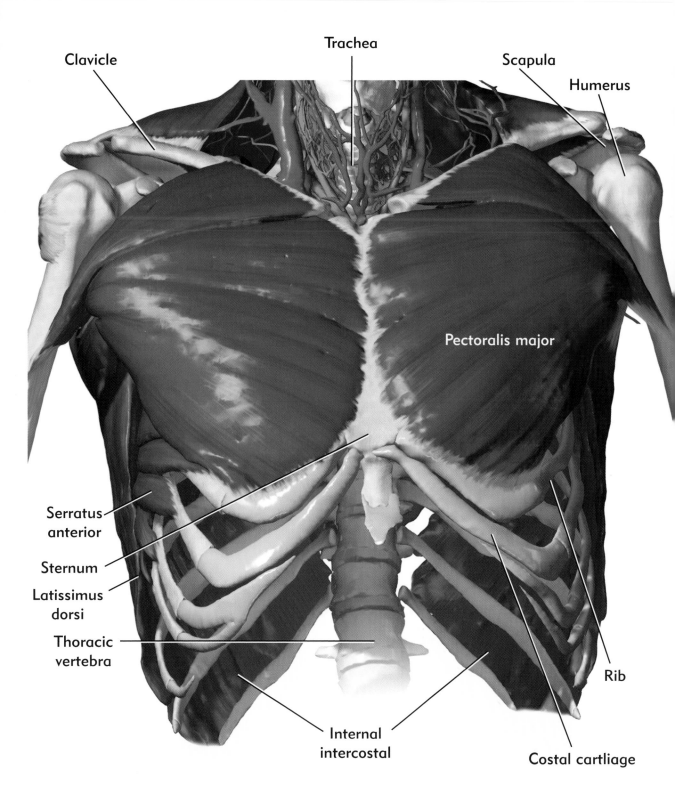

Clavicle

Trachea

Scapula

Humerus

Pectoralis major

Serratus anterior

Sternum

Latissimus dorsi

Thoracic vertebra

Internal intercostal

Costal cartliage

Rib

When you breathe in, the chest cavity expands. Muscles pull the ribs apart, and the diaphragm (not shown here) moves downward.

receive a message from the brain to contract. The diaphragm moves down from its normal resting position and flattens out near the bottom of the thoracic cavity, pushing on the lower ribs just enough to force them slightly out. At the same time, the intercostal muscles pull the upper ribs and sternum (the breastplate) in an upward and outward direction. It all sounds fairly complex, but the result is simple: the size of the chest increases.

Because the lungs are essentially "stuck" to the inside chest wall by their pleural layers, when the chest expands it stretches the lungs out with it. And when this happens, all kinds of interesting things take place. For one, the gases contained in the lungs spread out to fill the bigger space, resulting in a decrease in pressure. The pressure decreases so much, in fact, that it quickly becomes lower than that of the air outside the body.

Gases tend to move from areas of higher pressure to areas of lower pressure, so the higher-pressure air from outside the body—especially right around the nose and mouth—is suddenly drawn into the body, a lot like dirt being sucked in by a vacuum cleaner. Air, and whatever else is in it—dust, pollen, smoke, small bugs, you name it—rushes in through the mouth and nose. There, in a split second, it's prepped for delivery to the lungs. Bugs and other large objects are snagged by nasal hairs or caught by the tongue. Soot and dust are filtered out by a sticky layer of warm, moist mucus. The air itself is, thanks to the mucus, heated and humidified.

From the back of the nose or the mouth (depending on how you breathe—through your nose, your mouth, or both), the air continues down through the pharynx, is directed into the trachea, and splits left and right at the bronchi. The air that rushes into the right bronchus heads to the right lung, while that in the left bronchus heads for the left lung.

Normal Breathing

You can tell how your breathing is going by counting the number of times you breathe every minute. Most healthy adults, when they're not exercising, take twelve to twenty breaths per minute. Children tend to breathe more, around fifteen to thirty times per minute. Infants breathe most often. Their normal range is anywhere from twenty-five to fifty breaths per minute. When you watch a person breathe, you can see his or her chest expand with every inhalation and shrink with every exhalation. Count one inhalation plus one exhalation as one full breath. Many factors can influence respiration, and what is normal for one person may not be normal for the next. Your size, sex, age, and physical conditioning all play important roles in how often you breathe.

Inside of each lung, the air continues on its way. It travels from the bronchi into the bronchioles, and on to what scientists call the "respiratory zone." The respiratory zone is where the real breathing process—gas exchange—takes place. The zone includes narrow passageways called respiratory bronchioles; alveolar ducts, which act like connecting pipes to alveolar sacs; and alveolar sacs, which anchor clusters of tiny, hollow, grape-like alveoli. Gas exchange is when oxygen enters the bloodstream, and carbon dioxide and other waste gases enter the lungs. It occurs through the extremely thin walls of the alveoli. (For a description of the process, see the next chapter.)

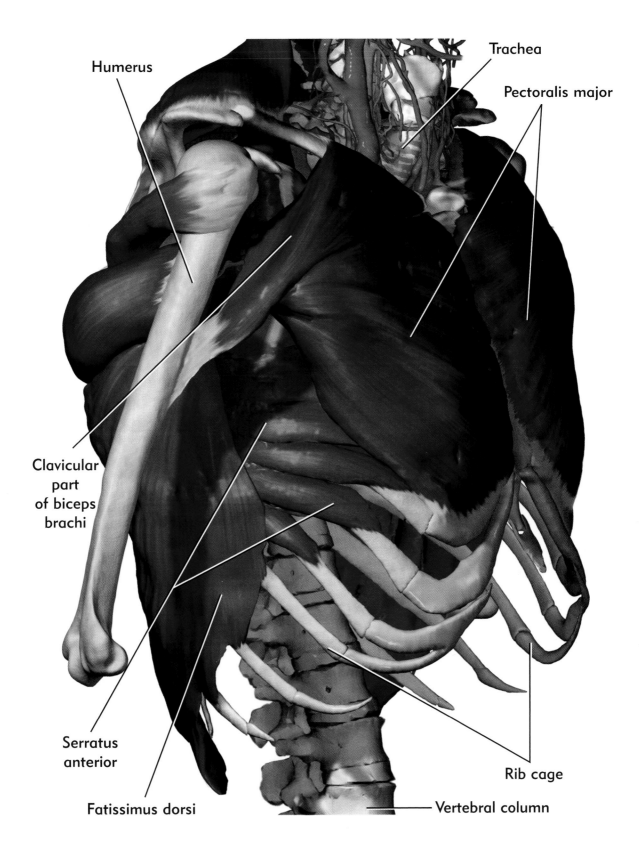

Humerus

Trachea

Pectoralis major

Clavicular
part
of biceps
brachi

Serratus
anterior

Fatissimus dorsi

Rib cage

Vertebral column

An anterolateral (front and side) view of the muscles of the thorax. The thorax contains the heart and lungs, and is well protected by the rib cage.

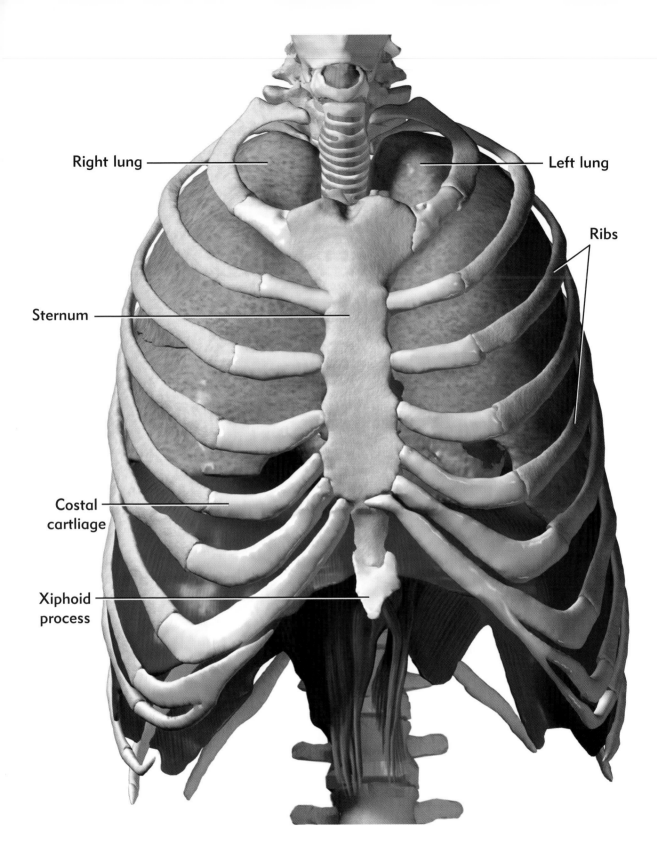

Right lung

Left lung

Ribs

Sternum

Costal cartliage

Xiphoid process

This is an anterior (front) view of the rib cage and lungs. The lungs are surrounded by membranes called pleurae, which form sacs or cavities around each lung. The cavities contain a lubricating fluid.

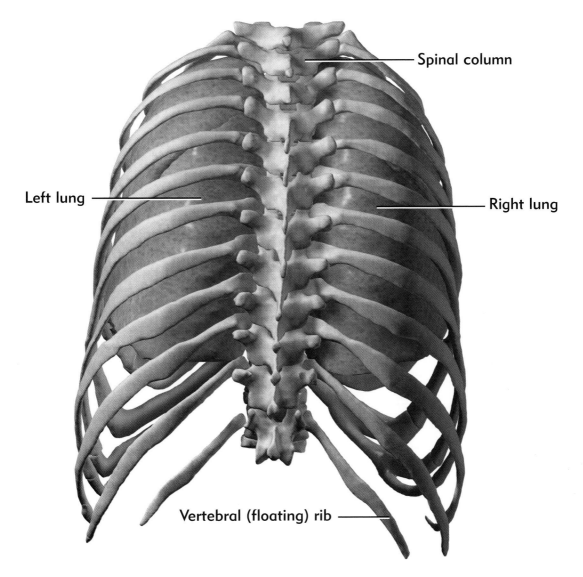

Spinal column

Left lung

Right lung

Vertebral (floating) rib

This posterior (rear) view of the rib cage reveals how well the ribs protect the lungs.

At the very end of the inhalation process, when your lungs feel full, the pressure within them is equal to the pressure of air in the atmosphere outside of the body. When this state occurs, the respiratory muscles, their jobs done, start to relax. Exhalation, or expiration, begins.

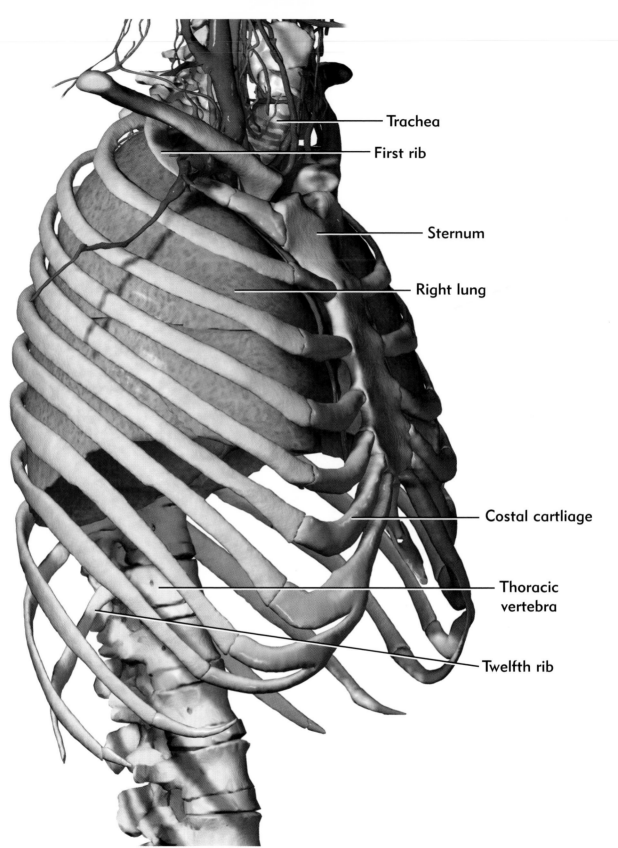

An anterolateral view of the thorax and rib cage with the muscles removed. There are twelve pairs of ribs attached to the thoracic vertebrae.

The exhalation process is the opposite of inhalation. The diaphragm moves up and the ribs and sternum move down and back to their normal resting positions, decreasing the size of the thoracic cavity. As the chest space narrows, so does the space within the lungs. Eventually, because of the squeezing, the pressure of the gases in the lungs becomes higher than the atmospheric pressure outside the body. Then, because gases tend to move from areas of higher pressure to areas of lower pressure, the higher-pressure gas inside the lungs is forced out of the body. Up and out it goes, retracing—in reverse—exactly the same route the air took on the way in.

Even after exhalation, a small amount of air remains in the lungs. You can try all you want to "blow" this air out of your body, but you won't succeed. Why? Well, the answer has to do with the body's need for a continuous supply of oxygen. If

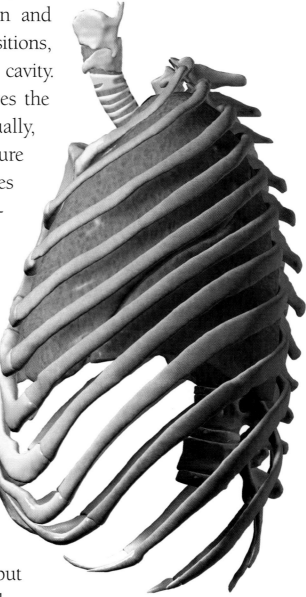

The ribs are flat bones that curve forward and downward toward the front of the body.

you were to get rid of all the air in your lungs, gas exchange could no longer take place and oxygen would not make it to the cells. And that, of course, could prove deadly. This extra residual volume of air essentially enables your body to continue breathing between actual breaths.

As you can see, the breathing process is mostly beyond our conscious control. But we can influence breathing to some extent. Remember when you tried to keep from inhaling at the beginning of this chapter? You were able to delay breathing for at most a few seconds. When you hold your breath, that's exactly what you're doing: putting the breathing process on temporary hold. You also influence your breathing, whether intentionally or not, when you talk, cough, sneeze, hiccup, or exercise. Think about it—the last time you ran as fast as you could go, what was your breathing like when you finally stopped?

Still, when it comes to breathing, there's no doubt who's in charge: your body, and your respiratory system in particular. So the next time you find yourself thinking about your breathing, relax. Let nature do its job.

THE LUNGS AND THE HEART

The heart, a muscular, fist-sized organ located between the lungs, is your personal blood pump. Through regular, well-timed contractions of its various components, it sends blood to every part of your body.

Not surprisingly, the incredibly important job of the respiratory system—to supply the entire body with the oxygen it needs to survive—would be absolutely impossible without blood and the heart. You can think of blood as a liquid taxicab. It picks up oxygen from the lungs, drives through the heart, and then zooms away to the rest of the body, dropping off enough oxygen at each cell to sustain life. Meanwhile, it picks up carbon dioxide and other waste products that you don't need and drives them to the lungs where they can be exhaled out of the body.

The heart's job in this process is to pump the blood where it needs to go. But to truly understand how the heart works, you must also know how it's built. The heart has two main divisions, right and left, and consists of four major chambers, two on the right and two on the left. The upper chambers on each side of the heart are called the atria. The lower chambers are known as ventricles. The muscle-bound chambers, through which all blood flows, do the actual pumping.

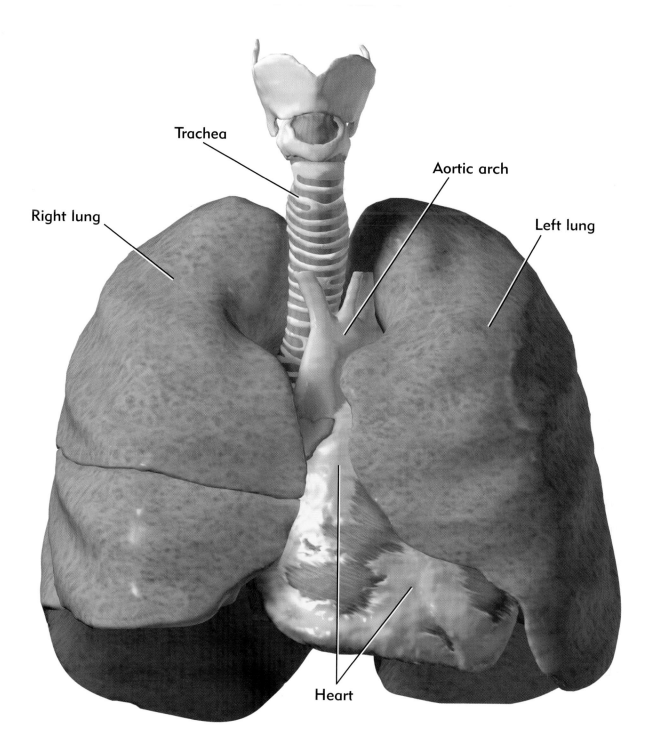

Trachea

Aortic arch

Right lung

Left lung

Heart

This image of the lungs shows the heart and the cardiac notch. Fatty tissue covers the surface of the heart, protecting the coronary arteries.

Here's how it works: blood that is low in oxygen but high in carbon dioxide enters the heart at the right atrium through big blood vessels called venae cavae. This blood contains very little oxygen because it dumped most of it at the body's cells. It also holds a lot of carbon dioxide because carbon dioxide is a natural by-product of metabolism, the process by which cells use oxygen to convert food into energy. The deoxygenated blood is pumped down and into the right ventricle through a one-way valve, then out of the heart and to the lungs through a major vessel called the pulmonary artery. The pulmonary artery is the only artery in the body that carries deoxygenated blood. As the pulmonary artery enters the lungs, it branches into smaller vessels called arterioles. Finally, it branches again, this time into even smaller blood vessels known as capillaries. The capillaries are microscopically thin—so thin, in fact, that they're perfect for gas exchange. In the lungs, they drape like webs over the alveoli.

Gas exchange in the lungs, called external respiration or pulmonary gas exchange, involves the actual swapping of gases between the alveoli and the blood. As you know, during inspiration oxygen-rich air enters and fills the millions of alveoli scattered throughout the lungs. But the oxygen does no good when it's stuck inside the alveoli. For it to be of any use, it must be transferred to the blood and transported to the rest of the body. And that's where the capillaries come into play.

Remember—the blood in the capillaries is very low in oxygen and very high in carbon dioxide. And the air in the alveoli is high in oxygen and low in carbon dioxide. Because gases tend to move from areas of high concentration to areas of low concentration, this setup proves perfect for a swap. Oxygen in the alveoli passes through the thin capillary walls and into the bloodstream, where it hitches a ride by attaching to special molecules called hemoglobin. At the same time, carbon dioxide leaves the capillaries and enters the alveoli. The blood in the

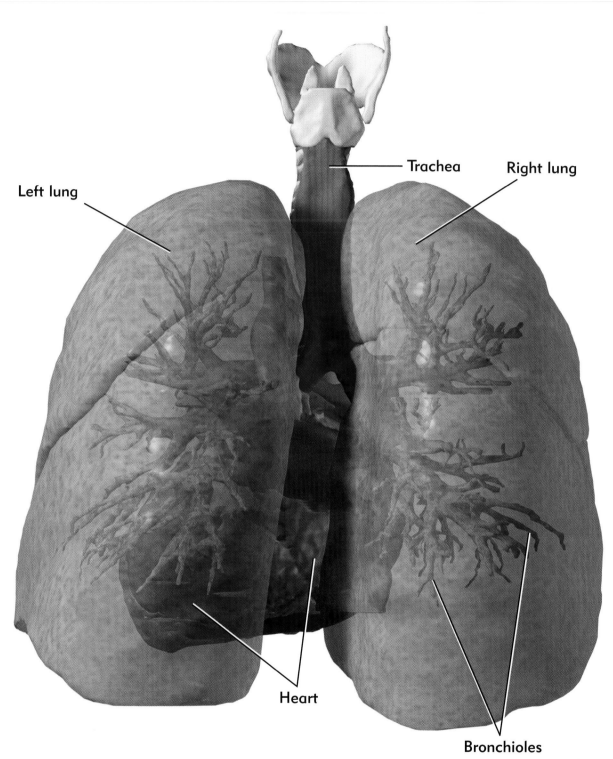

Left lung

Trachea

Right lung

Heart

Bronchioles

A posterior view of the lungs, trachea, and heart. The tissue of the lungs resembles a sponge and contains hundreds of millions of tiny air sacs, called alveoli.

capillaries, which is now rich with oxygen, continues on its way. And upon exhalation the carbon dioxide in the alveoli is ejected out of the body and into the air.

The newly oxygenated blood now heads back to the heart. The capillaries merge into larger vessels called venules, the venules lead to pulmonary veins, and the pulmonary veins enter the heart at the left atrium. The heart's job at this point is simple: send the oxygen-rich blood out to all the body's cells. Wasting no time, it directs the blood down into the left ventricle through another one-way valve, and with a swift, muscular contraction, pumps it out of the heart through the aortic artery.

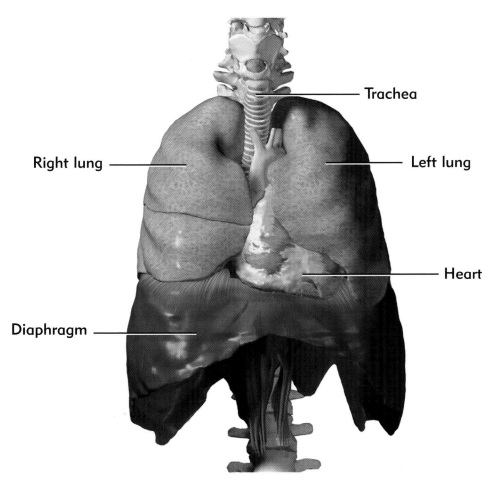

Trachea

Right lung

Left lung

Heart

Diaphragm

The average person takes between twelve and eighteen breaths per minute.

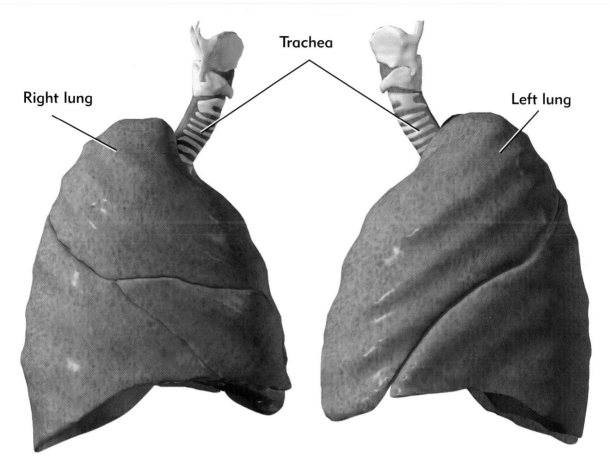

Trachea

Right lung

Left lung

Each lung resembles a large, pink sponge, and each is composed of a fine network of blood vessels and air sacs.

The aorta is the heart's main artery. It supplies all other arteries in the body with high-oxygen blood. Those arteries include the coronary arteries, which give the heart its blood supply; the carotid arteries, which lead up the neck and to the head and brain; the femoral arteries, which are in the thighs and legs; the brachial arteries, in the upper arms; and the radial arteries, in the lower arms. Other arteries lead elsewhere in the body. You can feel blood as it squeezes through the arteries when you take a pulse. Try checking your own radial pulse by placing three fingers on the palm-side of your wrist, right beneath your thumb.

The arteries eventually branch into smaller arterioles, then branch again into capillaries, which are found in every part of the body. At this point, another episode of gas exchange must take place in order to send oxygen out of the blood and into the body's cells. This swap, known as internal respiration, is the gas-exchange process that occurs between the capillaries and the cells that they cover.

Internal respiration is similar to the process that takes place in the lungs, only this time, the process is reversed. The blood in the capillaries surrounding the body's cells is saturated with oxygen that it picked up from the lungs. However, it is very low on carbon dioxide. The cells, on the other hand, are loaded with carbon dioxide but lacking oxygen. The gases, as usual, move from areas of high concentration to areas of low concentration. Oxygen passes through the thin capillary membrane and into the cells, while

The Cycle Continues

You may wonder just what happens to all the carbon dioxide that you expel into the air every time you exhale. Fortunately, at least some of it is put to use. In fact, plants love it. Plants absorb carbon dioxide from the air in a process called photosynthesis. With the aid of sunlight and water, special molecules in plants called chlorophyll convert carbon dioxide into useful com-pounds that are essential for growth. So the next time you find yourself breathing with nothing else to do, stroll over to a houseplant and give it some CO_2!

carbon dioxide passes out of the cells and into the capillary bloodstream. The blood, now high in carbon dioxide and low in oxygen, travels from the capillaries to larger venules, from venules to larger veins, into the venae cavae, and back into the heart. The heart, of course, directs the blood into the pulmonary vein and out to the lungs to start the whole process again.

4

OXYGEN AND METABOLISM

Everything you do—whether you're running a marathon, walking to class, sleeping, or even just breathing—requires energy. You need energy to stand and get out of bed, to chew and digest your breakfast, and to lift your backpack and swing it over your shoulder. Believe it or not, you even need energy to pump the blood in your heart all the way down your body and into your toes. Energy is vital for every single aspect of life.

If you like to eat, energy is not exactly hard to come by. You get your energy from food—everything from pasta to chicken to fish to fruits and vegetables. You might wonder just how it is that the human body is able to take something as basic as an apple and turn it into something useful, like the energy to hammer a nail or lift a heavy book. The answer has to do with a complicated chemical process called metabolism.

The conversion of food into energy begins with digestion, when most nutrients are absorbed into the bloodstream through the intestines and into the intestinal capillaries. Once the nutrients enter the bloodstream, a vein carries them to the liver. From there, the nutrients are transported to cells throughout the body. Cells pick up the nutrients in almost the same way they accumulate oxygen. The nutrients move from areas of higher concentration in the blood to areas of low concentration in the cells. Once the nutrients are in the cells, the metabolic process begins.

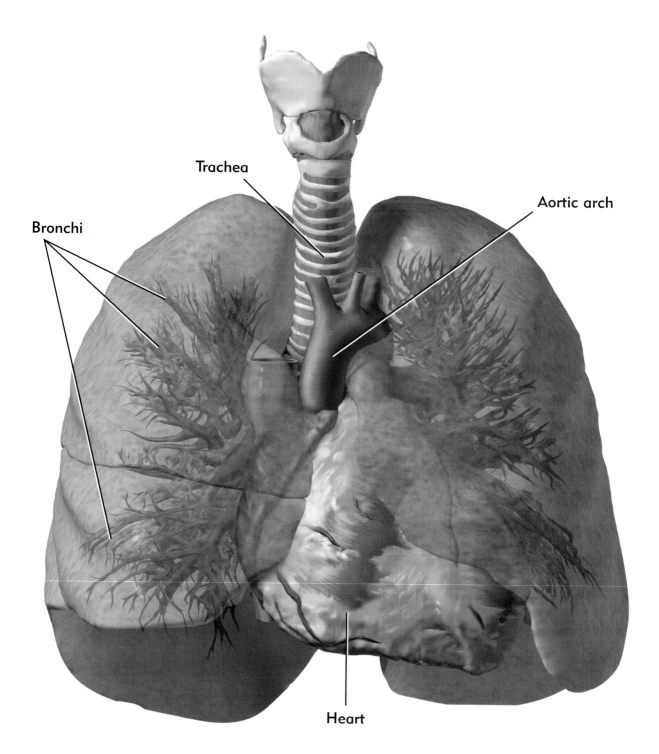

Bronchi

Trachea

Aortic arch

Heart

This anterior view of the lungs clearly shows the network of bronchi, or air passages, that reach into all areas of the lungs.

Out of Breath?

If you've ever wondered why you breathe so hard when you're running or biking up a hill, here's why. You're burning through your adenosine triphosphate (ATP) and your cells are begging for oxygen so they can make more. By breathing harder—an act that you cannot control in this instance—your body is taking in more air and sending the oxygen from that air to your muscles.

A similar thing happens at high altitudes. Because there is less oxygen in the air at high altitudes, people from sea level who travel to places above 7,000 feet often find themselves out of breath every time they move. Again, their bodies are telling them they need more oxygen for metabolism and force them to breathe more air as a result.

Of course, in both of these examples it's not hard to overcome the need to breathe hard. All you have to do is train your body. In the case of problems breathing at high altitudes, the best plan of attack is gradual acclimatization. When you acclimatize, you spend enough time at a high altitude to allow your body to adjust to the low oxygen levels. When you do so, your body naturally develops more and more red blood cells—the cells that carry oxygen. This increases your body's ability to take in and transport oxygen to the muscles that need them.

When it comes to that hill, on the other hand, the best thing to do is get in shape. If you can build the specific muscles involved in running or biking, for example, you'll increase the amount of mitochondria within them. And the more mitochondria you have, the better your muscles will be at converting nutrients into energy.

The word "metabolism," when used in science, refers to all the chemical and energy changes that occur in the body. More specifically, it refers to the ability of the body's cells to take oxygen from the lungs and use it to help convert carbohydrates, fat, and protein from food into the high-energy chemical compound ATP, or adenosine triphosphate. When a food item as simple as a potato, for example, is eaten, digested, delivered to the body's cells as nutrients, and then combined with oxygen (oxidized) to make ATP, those cells can take that energy and use it immediately to do work.

Oxidation of food nutrients and the production of ATP occur only in specialized cellular parts called mitochondria. Some cells have more mitochondria than others. The more mitochondria a cell has, the greater its ability to produce ATP.

The rate at which our cells metabolize food is what determines how much oxygen those cells need. When we're sitting around doing nothing, or sleeping, the oxygen needs of our cells are at their lowest. At times like this, our blood can easily deliver enough oxygen to the cells for metabolism to proceed. During exercise, however, when we're burning up our energy at a much faster rate, we need much more oxygen—ten to twenty times as much as that which we need at rest. The more work our muscles do, the more the cells in those muscles need additional ATP.

When your muscles are first used following rest, they hold enough ATP reserves to fuel activity for a few seconds. But once this ATP is used up, new ATP must be made. At first, chemicals in the bloodstream get additional ATP by breaking down a compound stored in the muscles called creatine phosphate. But again, after a few seconds of muscular activity, the supply runs out. At this point, the body must get ATP through metabolism.

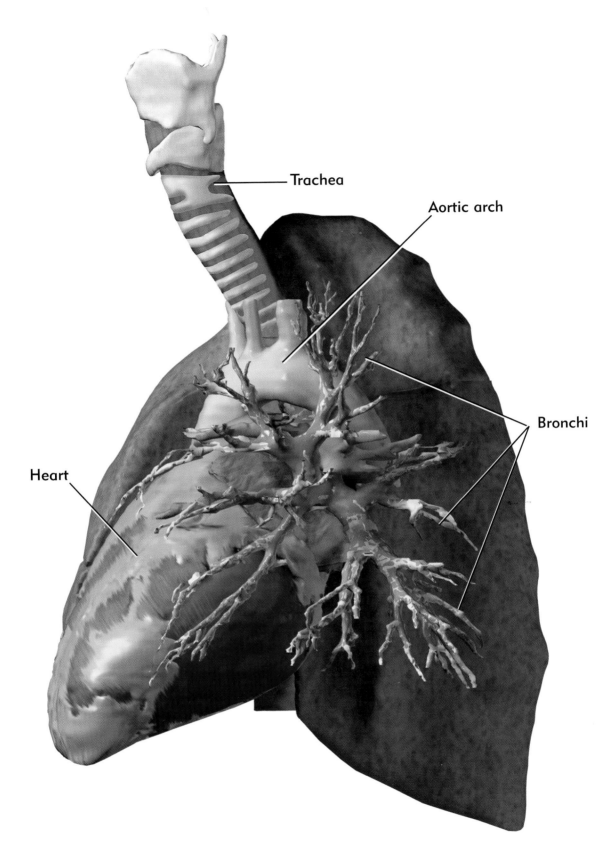

Trachea

Aortic arch

Bronchi

Heart

The branching air passages of the left lung are visible in this image.

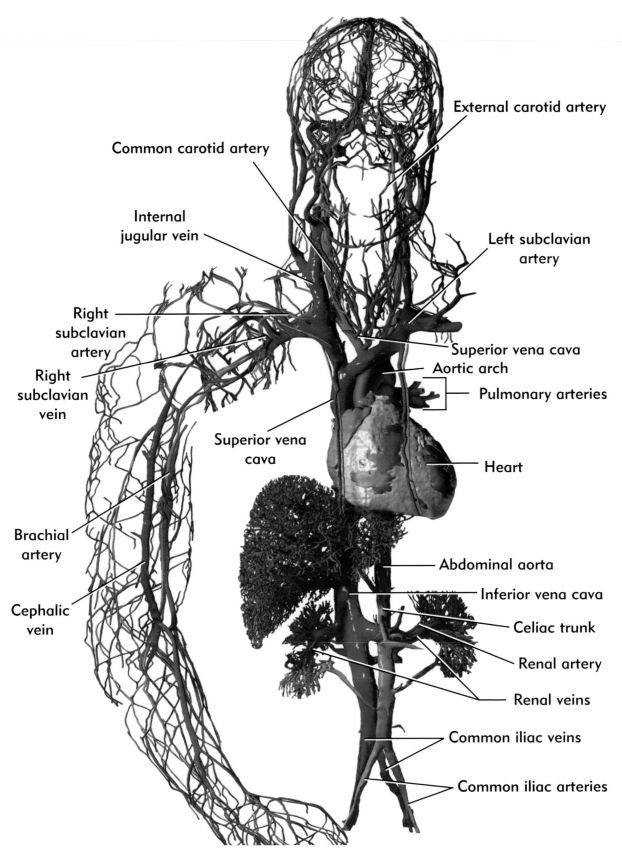

External carotid artery

Common carotid artery

Internal jugular vein

Left subclavian artery

Right subclavian artery

Right subclavian vein

Superior vena cava

Aortic arch

Pulmonary arteries

Superior vena cava

Heart

Brachial artery

Cephalic vein

Abdominal aorta

Inferior vena cava

Celiac trunk

Renal artery

Renal veins

Common iliac veins

Common iliac arteries

The arterial system of the upper body. The heart pumps blood to the lungs, where it picks up oxygen before it is pumped through the body.

Highly conditioned athletes can train their respiratory and cardiovascular systems to take in and use oxygen at extremely high rates—much higher than the average couch potato. Still, even the best athletes eventually reach a point where their oxygen intake is not enough to satisfy their metabolic needs. This can happen for a number of reasons, including the inability of the heart to pump an adequate amount of blood at a rate fast enough to deliver oxygen to the muscles that need it. When this happens, metabolism becomes anaerobic—that is, it occurs without oxygen. Anaerobic metabolism is not nearly as efficient as aerobic metabolism in converting food compounds into energy. The result of anaerobic metabolism is that waste products from the metabolic process accumulate in the bloodstream. Eventually the waste products, especially lactic acid, limit the athlete's ability to use his or her muscles. If you've ever felt a severe burning feeling in your legs from running very fast for a long period of time, or hiking or biking up a steep hill, you know exactly what an accumulation of lactic acid feels like.

Aerobic metabolism results in waste products, too, especially carbon dioxide and water. But unlike lactic acid, carbon dioxide and water are both easily eliminated from the body when we exhale.

GLOSSARY

anatomy   Study of the structure of the body and all of its parts.

atmospheric pressure   Pressure of the air outside of the body.

blood vessels   Arteries, veins, capillaries, and other pipe-like parts of the body used in the circulation of blood.

carbon dioxide   Naturally occurring gas that is a by-product of metabolism.

deoxygenated blood   Blood that is low in or lacking oxygen.

exhalation (expiration) Breathing out.

external respiration   Gas-exchange process that occurs between capillaries and the alveoli in the lungs.

gas exchange   Process by which two or more gases change places.

inhalation (inspiration)   Breathing in.

intercostal muscles   Muscles located between each rib.

internal respiration   Gas-exchange process that occurs between capillaries and the body's cells.

interpleural space   Area between pleural layers in the lungs.

membrane   Thin layer of body tissue.

metabolism   Chemical changes in cells that produce energy necessary for life.

oxygen   Naturally occurring gas found in air that is vital for all life.

oxygenated blood   Blood that has oxygen in it.

parietal pleura   Layer of tissue that lines the internal chest walls.

pulmonary artery   Artery in the body that carries oxygenated blood from the heart to the lungs.

respiration   Process by which oxygen and carbon dioxide are exchanged during breathing.

respiratory system   Organs in the body involved in breathing.

respiratory zone   Part of the respiratory system that includes the respiratory bronchioles, alveolar ducts, alveolar sacs, and alveoli.

thoracic cavity   The internal space in the chest.

visceral pleura   Layer of tissue that is attached to the lungs.

FOR MORE INFORMATION

Organizations

American Lung Association

1740 Broadway

New York, NY 10019

(212) 315-8700

Web site: http://www.lungusa.org

This group offers information on lung disease and disease prevention.

American Medical Association

515 North State Street

Chicago, IL 60610

(312) 464-5000

Web site: http://www.ama-assn.org

Canadian Lung Association

3 Raymond Street, Suite 300

Ottawa, ON K1R 1A3

(613) 569-6411

Web site: http://www.lung.ca

The association's Web site includes information for kids.

National Heart, Lung, and Blood Institute
National Institutes of Health
P.O. Box 30105
Bethesda, MD 20824-0105
(301) 592-8573
Web site: http://www.nhlbi.nih.gov
The NIH is the U.S. Department of Health and Human Services'
main agency for medical research, and is one of the world's most
important research centers.

Web Sites

Anatomy-Resources.com
http://www.anatomy-resources.com
This site is a great place to find cool anatomy books and models of
body parts, skeletons, and organs.

Association of Anatomists
http://www.anatomy.org/anatomy/nresource.htm
This site contains a list of anatomy resources available on the Internet.

BodyQuest
http://library.thinkquest.org/10348/home.html
Take a tour of the virtual human body and learn about its different
systems at this Web site.

HealthWeb
http://www.healthweb.org
This site has links to health information available on the Internet.

How Stuff Works

http://www.howstuffworks.com/lung

This site has an easy-to-follow explanation of how the lungs work.

KidsHealth

http://www.kidshealth.org

This site has information and fun games about health and the human body, including the lungs.

FOR FURTHER READING

Alcamo, Edward. *Anatomy and Physiology the Easy Way.* Hauppauge,
    NY: Barrons Educational Series, 1996.

Clayman, Charles. *Illustrated Guide to the Human Body.* New York:
    DK Publishing, 1995.

Furgang, Kathy. *My Lungs.* New York: PowerKids Press, 2001.

Kapit, Wynn. *The Anatomy Coloring Book.* Reading, MA: Addison-
    Wesley Publishing Company, 1993.

Parker, Steve. *Eyewitness: The Human Body.* New York:
    DK Publishing, 1999.

Parker, Steve. *Lungs.* Brookfield, CT: Copper Beech Books, 1996.

Stille, Darlene. *The Respiratory System.* Danbury, CT:
    Children's Press, 1998.

INDEX

About the Author

Chris Hayhurst is an emergency medical technician, professional author, and journalist with more than a dozen books and hundreds of articles in print. He lives and works in Fort Collins, Colorado.

Photo Credits

All digital images courtesy of Visible Productions, by arrangement with Anatographica, LLC.

Series Design

Claudia Carlson

Layout

Tahara Hasan